Dear Auntie Rottie
Canine Agony Aunt

Sue Barr Cochrane

Acknowledgements

M. Downward	Editor

Photography

Kate Ziecik	Rocco
Lisa Edwards	Harvey
The Kenyon Family	Lucy
Fiona McHugh	Bella
Fiona McHugh	Hens

"The Bubble-Gum Machine" cartoon by Martyn Dey

Forward

A few years ago my sister, Liz Ashworth, cookery writer for the Knock News (now known as the KN) suggested to the Editor, David Gordon, it might be a novel idea to feature an article for dog lovers. He agreed and so Dear Auntie Rottie Canine Agony Aunt was born. I wrote a monthly column for several years collecting a vast range of interesting and amusing information.

Friends and customers suggested that it would be a great idea to publish some of these letters.

So, here they are, folks! Read on.................

Sue Barr Cochrane was born in 1953 and grew up in Elgin, Morayshire. From an early age, animals played a huge part in her life.

After leaving Elgin Academy, she pursues a course (BHSAI) in riding instruction and taught for several years in equestrian establishments where a passion for teaching evolved.

Sue's particular interest lay in helping children and adults overcome their fear and nervousness which prevented them from enjoying their hobby. She also gave her time and expertise to Riding for the Disabled. Through private instruction, she coached talented young riders to achieve their goals.

Roughly twenty years ago, and quite by chance, Sue turned her teaching and training skills towards helping dogs and their owners. She became a Chartered Member of the Institute of Animal Care Education and a Member of the Academy of Dog Training and Behaviour. Regardless of having letters to display after your name, Sue advocates that nothing counts for experience in the real world and learning is a lifelong process!

Psychological and physical well-being is of specific interest and well-ingrained in Sue's training methods, gleaned from close study of inter-canine communication and behaviour on a daily basis – her own dogs are a superb teachers! The application of her findings forms a unique style of training which brings about dramatic results for both dog and owner. She continues to be amazed by some of the truly remarkable outcomes.

On the strength of her excellent results as a trainer, the majority of Sue's work comes from customer recommendation, referrals from local veterinary practitioners and rescue societies. Forever passionate about her work she runs her successful training business under the name of "It's a Dog's Life" based in Cummingston, Moray.

Contents   Page

Dear Auntie Rottie,

I am not a dog owner, but I often go out on walks with a friend who has a dog. For the best part of these walks, the tracks and paths are fine and a pleasure to walk along. I am amazed to see so many poo bags left hanging on branches, on the wayside and believe it not, actually by the poo waste bins! It seems that pink and green poo bags are the favoured colours! Worst of all is poo just left on the tracks and paths – yuck! Why are some dog owners so inconsiderate? Love to hear what you have to say about it....

Yours sincerely,

Mrs Wright - Browned - Awf!

Kick It – Flick It – Bag It – Bin It!

Dear Mrs Wright-Browned-Awf!

There are thousands more dogs in the domestic environment than there were even a few years ago. Our dog is a much loved part of our family, but do we owners really take total responsibility for all aspects of our dog's care – including their *poo*?

Most dogs are desperate to empty themselves at the start of their walk. So, the first three to five hundred metres of a park or woodland walk is generally covered in dog deposits! In the height of summer, the stench, the malodour, the pong, the niffy whiffs of latrineous excrement – call it what you like – is eye-watering and downright offensive. There really is nothing quite like the feeling of knowing you have just stood in a dog *poo*!

We could, of course, train our dogs "to woopsy" in the garden before going on exercise. "Walkies" can, however, cause great excitement which often results in unexpected and large evacuations of the bowels!

The enormous variety of food available for different breeds and needs is truly mind-blowing. Having bought and paid for the all-singing, all-dancing, super-duper food, once our dog has digested the culinary delight, we still own, and are responsible for, the inevitable deposit of residue – *poo*!

Dog poo is a subject that causes much discussion and controversy, sometimes leading to heated arguments and, dare I say, *poo rage!*

The fact of the matter remains that our dog is our responsibility and when he's got to go, he's got to go. We have to pickit up and we must dispose of it appropriately! We are encouraged *to bag it and bin it.* Very often, however, there are no bins. Some owners are reluctant to cart around a smelly bag of poo. So, some of those owners leave the bag lying on the ground, or festooning a tree or dangling on a fence for later collection – except they generally forget or decide to take a different route home and the discarded poo bag remains to smell another day.

Some owners think that if the bag is hidden, that's OK.   Here's an example....

A groundsman at Duff House, Banff, once extricated one hundred and eighty three bags of dog poo from a large flower bed in the gardens. Perhaps one for the Guinness Book of Records?

Many estates are promoting "kick and flick". Dog owners are invited to *"kick and flick"* their dog's poo off the path. If you happen to own a very large dog, this could prove to be something of a challenge!

In remote areas that are not popular with regular dog walkers, that's all very well. It certainly beats *leaving* "*it*" as a "*roundabout*" in the middle of the path for the next unsuspecting walker to tread in.

"*Kicking and flicking*" at the local park or woods, however, isn't really an option, is it?

It's not as though poo bags cost anything. Ask in the local library or local shops where poo bags are completely free of charge. There is very little free in life, but poo bags are – just ask!

Auntie Rottie says

"Our dog(s) -our responsibility
His or her poo -   our responsibility!"

Dear Auntie Rottie,

Here is a picture of a puppy we saw last week. We would very much like to have her. Our friends advised us to approach you first for some sound and honest advice before we go ahead.

Look forward to hearing from you soon.

Hamish & Rachel Barker

Dear Hamish & Rachel,

So…you're thinking of getting a puppy? How exciting!

Do remember, owning a dog will require your total commitment for anything up to 18 years!

Do some thorough research!

The Kennel Club website will provides comprehensive and impartial information on the history, exercise and grooming needs, trainability and temperament of the breed you are considering.

www.thekennelclub.org.uk

Choose a breed that suits your lifestyle!

For example, if you live in a small flat it could be foolhardy to buy a Great Dane!

Have you enough time to regularly exercise and train **every day**? If you are out working fulltime, please think again!

Can you afford the feeding and veterinary costs? Apart from the expense of purchasing the puppy, the initial outlay includes buying an appropriate sized housecage, good quality food, bowls and bedding, grooming equipment, collar and lead, etc.

Veterinary costs include microchipping, annual vaccination, worming, neutering (if required) and any other treatment that may be needed.

Can you afford pet insurance? There are many companies offering pet insurance.

PLEASE READ THE SMALL PRINT!

OK, let's choose your puppy!

It would be wise to seek professional advice from a reputable dog trainer in your area. It's so important not to let your heart rule your head! All puppies are cute and cuddly, and all puppies will melt your heart....and your wallet!

Regardless of where the puppies have been reared, it is essential that they have been well handled. Exposure to domesticity, hearing the vacuum cleaner, telephone, hairdryer, doors banging, etc. at an early age is crucial for future development. Have they been out in the garden? You'd be surprised the number of puppies that don't know what grass is until they are 8 weeks old and going to their new homes.

Watch the puppies with their mother. Although they are now long weaned, there may be one pup that still thinks Mum is its property and makes this very plain to the rest of the litter. Possessive guarding of a resource (mum) is assertive behaviour and indicates this puppy might be a handful to train.

Watch the litter playing together.

Have you spotted which is the most headstrong of the puppies? If you're not sure what to look for, these are some of the signs: placing the head and neck, or paws, over the shoulders of another, mounting behaviour and generally being very bossy. This puppy is obviously very determined and could prove to be a challenge to train.

Is there one that goes off by itself, independently exploring and ignoring the advances of the others? An independent dog is very much his or her own person, sorry, dog, and can like bossy boots above, be challenging to train.

Is one displaying more submissiveness than the others by always giving in, rolling on its back and not offering any retaliation?

Does one sit in the corner looking "hang dog"?

Both of these could indicate a shy or nervous disposition. All things considered, and with a very large pinch of common sense, look for a good mixture of assertive and submissive behaviour.

If you decide to buy two puppies from the same litter, thinking they will be good company for each other, this might spell disaster for the future, particularly if they are same sex.

Remember dogs need hierarchy for peace to reign and if they are the same age, same sex, same temperament and same size, it can be extremely difficult to establish and maintain hierarchy between them. They may rub along quite nicely together, thank you, until they reach around 8 to 10 months at which point they suddenly start to fight. There is no solution to this littermate aggression other than to rehome one of them and that's a devastating decision to have to make!

Temperament Test

There are several simple tests you might like to try to get a good idea of a puppy's likely future temperament.

Take each puppy, away from the rest of the litter, one by one, preferably outside on to grass.

Pick up the puppy, turn it on its back and cradle it in your arms, just like you would with a baby. Ideally, after a short struggle the puppy should relax.

Next, place the palm of your hand under its tummy and support the chest with your index and middle fingers. Now lift the puppy just 2 or 3 inches off the ground. Once more, after a short struggle, the puppy should relax.

Now release the puppy and clap your hands loudly. What is the reaction? Look for interest and curiosity and not turning away in disinterest or backing away in fear.

Take an old glove with you. Tease the puppy with it and then toss the glove away from you. Does the puppy dash after it and with lots of encouragement bring it back to you? Does the puppy show complete disinterest and wander off? Does the puppy dash out, grab the glove and run off with it?

What do you think? I know which one I would choose! The one that brings my old glove back!

Encourage the puppy to follow and interact with you. If the puppy backs away in fear or ignores you, this may not be the one for you. Ideally you are looking for a puppy that wants to be with you and engage with you.

Now, after all the above, once the gene team's done its job, a puppy will be the product of its next environment – and that's down to *you*, the new owner! There are very many reputable breeders who care passionately about ensuring each of their puppies goes to the right home and the right owner. They provide a puppy pack with all the information you need to get started, a sample of the food to which the puppy has been weaned and very often several weeks free insurance, courtesy of The Kennel Club. Many breeders use a proviso which states that, should the new owner find they can no longer care for the dog, it must be returned to the breeder.

A Cautionary Note

Having sourced a litter – a word of warning....

If the breeder:

Produces one puppy at a time and will not let you see the litter.....

Will not let you see the mother – "because she's always a bit touchy when she has puppies"....

Won't let you handle the puppies....

The establishment is dirty and there are lots and lots of dogs and puppies....

These are not ideal conditions from which to choose your future canine companion. *Think again!*

If you suspect you may be at a puppy farm, please report your concerns to your local RSPCA. This can be done anonymously.

With very best wishes for the future.

Auntie Rottie Says............

"Don't delay start training today!"

The Puppy Santa brought me for Christmas….

Dear Auntie Rottie

Santa brought me a puppy for Christmas! She's a Labradoodle called Millie. She's 8 weeks old and I just adore her, but I really need help to solve some problems. Even though I leave the back door open for her to go out to the toilet, she just comes back in and does it on the carpet. Someone said to rub her nose in it but I think this is cruel. Is this what I should do? When I see her toileting in the house, I say "no" very loudly and she runs away. So she knows she is doing wrong.

The other thing I would like help with is Millie's biting. I'm worried she is going to be aggressive. Help!

From Diane

Dear Diane

Just as predicted! No sooner has your adorable little puppy arrived she starts peeing and pooing in the house and, of course, biting! Problems at both ends, I'd say!

Let's tackle the toileting issue. First, purchase a housecage, but not a great big one you think she'll grow into, otherwise she will use one end as her bedroom and the other as an ensuite! Pups don't like to soil their sleeping area and in the correct size of cage, Millie will learn to "hang on" – unless, of course, you leave her too long in which case she will be forced to wet her pants or worse!

The housecage will be her den and safe place. Introduce her to her den by feeding her in it. Put Millie in her cage at night, at **any** time she cannot be properly supervised, when you are eating or preparing food and for regular periods of time throughout the day.

Your puppy already knows how to toilet, Diane, but she doesn't know where you want her to do it. By shouting "no" at her, you will frighten her. She will think you don't like to see her toileting and will, no doubt, hide away when she needs to go. To Millie, leaving the back door open only means she can come and go as she pleases.

So, if you catch your puppy starting to toilet in the house, please say nothing! Whisk her up in your arms and go out to the designated toileting area in the garden. If, having waited for a few minutes, Millie hasn't performed, quietly put her in her housecage. Only "empty" puppies may run around in the house.

As a general rule, Millie will need to toilet as soon as she wakens, not long after she has been fed, during play and at regular intervals during the day. Bear in mind that puppies often need to pee more than once, so be patient and wait a few minutes. Use a specific word e.g. "busy" or "go potty" as Millie is in the process of peeing or pooing. Eventually this will act as a trigger for toileting. Say it quietly! If you are too effusive, your pup will stop toileting and come to see why you are getting so excited.

Puppies, like babies, need a lot of sleep. Puppies, like babies, that do not have enough sleep are 'orrible!

Now guess what?.........puppies, like babies, need routine. So it's a good idea to put Millie in her den for a nap in the morning for a couple of hours at least and the same in the afternoon. Don't let her sleep just anywhere.

At this very young age, you can expect Millie to poo first thing in the morning or immediately after her breakfast and possibly three or four times more during the day. She will pee more frequently than poo.

Young pups' "plumbing" cannot last the night so until she is 9 to 10 weeks old, you will need to set your alarm clock for 2 or 3am, and gradually later, to take her out to toilet.

When you brought Millie home, she'd been plucked away from her brothers and sisters. To lessen the impact of this dramatic change, for the first few nights, have her housecage in your bedroom. I recommend you cover the housecage completely – just like shutting your curtains! It will be a comfort for her to hear your breathing (or snoring!) and to know she hasn't been completely abandoned. You will hear Millie if she needs to go out to the toilet and you will quickly recognise the difference between *"wanting out"* and *"wanting attention".* Quite soon Millie will be able to last all night and you can gradually move the house cage to where it will be for the next few months.

Millie is biting and mouthing! That's wonderful news! Don't worry, she isn't being aggressive. She is doing exactly what Mother Nature intended her to do. Millie was born with needles for teeth in underdeveloped jaws.

Puppies need to learn to control their "armoury" before they are fully grown with lovely big white teeth in fully developed jaws. If Millie hasn't been, or has been prevented from, learning to control her teeth and jaws by then, we could have a problem.

In the litter environment, puppies play-fight constantly amid trips to mum's milk bar, sleeping and toileting. If one pup sinks its teeth in just a little too hard, its brother or sister will yelp loudly. Some pups think this is great and "attack" again with even more gusto – a bully in the pack! The recipient will squeal again and move away from his or her "assailant", refusing to play until some appeasing gesture has been delivered by the offender – a lick on the face ("sorry!"), a yawn ("calm down dear, I didn't mean it, honest!"), a front paw raise ("please, can I be your friend?") or a play bow ("would you like to chase me?"). The lesson learnt is that if you are a bully you end up playing on your own – *Billy No-Mates* – and that's the end of the world!

In a domestic environment, when a puppy becomes part of the human pack, suddenly feedback from littermates stops.

If Millie nips or bites you, please do not use old fashioned punishments such as a rolled up newspaper or a smack on the nose. Such barbaric actions will certainly not promote a soft and gentle mouth. You will, however, teach your puppy that you are not very nice at all, a horrible playmate and, indeed, really scary to be near!

By giving feedback in the way Nature intended, Millie will continue learn the lesson that began with her brothers and sisters. Firstly, home in on the hardest of the "bites" – yelp "ooooyah!" Take your hand away and act really hurt. Millie may react by pulling her ears back, frantically licking her lips or your hands while making herself look smaller. In puppy talk that's appeasement – "oooh, sorry Mum, got it wrong!"

If you have a little monster that thinks this is a good game and comes in for a second round, again, yelp loudly and abruptly leave the room. This means - *"I'm not playing with you any more, you don't play fair!"*

Wait 20 or 30 seconds and upon re-entering the room quietly call your puppy to you. Gently take her collar under her chin and stroke over the top of her head. *"Millie, are we friends again?* Please remember *"I'm in charge around here."*

The response from your pup will dictate your next move, Diane. Pups hate to be left alone and now, Millie, no doubt, will be very pleased to see you, licking your hands and gazing adoringly up at you.

If, on the other (bleeding) hand Millie sees it as another opportunity to perform further surgical procedures, abruptly leave the room and repeat the process.

You may be wondering what havoc your puppy is wreaking while you are in the hallway nursing your wounds.

There are two alternatives:

Make sure there are no delightful puppy magnet ornaments, newspapers, magazines, shoes, etc. lying around or anything that might invite destruction. Otherwise, use the housecage for time out.

This latter option is preferable, providing it is done very carefully. Millie's housecage must *never* be used as a place of punishment. The housecage must *always* be her safe place. It does, however serve as a useful place for her to cool her jets..

So, instead of leaving the room when Millie is too enthusiastic with her needles, gently and silently pick her up and put her in her housecage. Leave her there for 20 or 30 seconds *or* until she is quiet. Then silently release her from her den. When she is calm, quietly call her to you, take her collar under her chin and gently stroke her over her head.

If she erupts into a little biting machine again, it may well be that, just like babies, she is overtired and needs a nap in her housecage. Do also remember, an overexcited puppy will be almost uncontrollable – and whose fault's that?

There is a time in the day, very often around 6 or 7pm when the majority of puppies *"run the wall of death"*, racing around at the speed of sound with ears flapping and bottoms tucked in, being thoroughly silly and completely out of control. The technical term for this is *"crepuscular"*. Try to channel this energy into a game in the garden but if your pup is sailing at 10,000 feet, it's probably advisable to quietly retire him/her to the housecage for chill time. As soon as Millie has had all of her vaccinations, do some research and take her along to a reputable training and socialisation class.

Have fun!

Auntie Rottie

Dogs' Day Out

Fun in the river

Dear Auntie Rottie

Rosie, the Border Terrier, whom I have known all her seven years, was loaned to me by my daughter in November on the day after my 12 year-old Lab-collie Floss died, partly of a broken heart two months after my husband's death. Rosie was such a ray of sunshine at that sad time that I have unwisely left the following noisy hunting unchecked.

Rosie spends the bonnie days out in the back garden, hunting pretend vermin under the cypress hedge. The main problem with this is that she accompanies the digging with high-pitched yelps of aggression or triumph, as she pounces on the offending 'vermin'.

She makes the pretence more realistic by throwing my ornamental, beach-collected pebbles from the path-edge into the hedge throwing them hither and thither, to the danger of the greenhouse, once she runs them to earth. The second problem is her chewing the lower branches off the hedge to facilitate the finding, and the third problem, she has got me trained to come at a certain kind of bark at the back door and throw the pebbles she has placed on the doorstep.

How do I discourage this irritating yelping as she hunts phantom vermin?

Phyllis Goodhall

Imaginary Friends

Dear Phyllis

Rosie the Border Terrier certainly has got you very well trained. But she has, as you say, been a little ray of sunshine since the death of your husband, playing a crucial part in your life at this difficult time.

It's not surprising that you have allowed the behaviours you describe to go unchecked; it is easy to become emotionally dependent on our canine friends whose love is so unconditional. If you have neighbours, however, I am sure they do not appreciate the daily hunt with its attendant sound effects.

This is a very difficult "prey" behaviour to control. Terriers are natural hunters, especially for small prey such as mice or voles.

Rosie is like a child with an imaginary friend – she has imaginary "vermin"!

First of all, you must restrict her time in the garden to supervised freedom only, preferably on a lead or long line, this to break the focus on "the hunt". She must also have plenty of exercise, three good walks daily if you are able. On walks, play "hide and seek", change direction without telling her and give huge praise when she "hunts" you out. In the house, hide toys and treats for her so she still has the thrill of the "hunt".

The following you will find difficult but to establish your leadership:

Ignore attention seeking by turning your back on Rosie.

Keep a favourite toy that **you** take out to play with her, rather than Rosie coming to you with a toy and telling you when to play.

Call her to you frequently to give her a cuddle – this being the opposite of Rosie coming to you to demand a cuddle!

When you have been away from her, ignore her completely until she is calm, then call her and make a big fuss.

By keeping control of her activity in the garden and giving her alternatives, Rosie should remain that wonderful ray of sunshine but without the sound effects!

Auntie Rottie

Humphrey

Dear Auntie Rottie

My name is Humphrey. I'm a chocolate Labrador and though I say it myself, I'm a very handsome chap.

Recently, I celebrated my 1st birthday. As you might imagine, I am adored by my owner and her friends. I was showered with gifts of new toys and packets of treats.

What a lucky birthday boy I am!

I fairly tucked into the yummy treats, but quite quickly I began to feel not a little odd. I found myself feeling agitated and unable to settle for my usual afternoon snooze.

If that wasn't bad enough, I began to feel itchy. To my great embarrassment the word "fleas" was mentioned. To top it all, I started passing wind! My owner, Jane, is beside herself thinking that I've not only picked up a tummy bug, but also an infestation of fleas.

Oh the shame of it!

We had a discreet appointment with my vet – I would not like my friends to learn of my predicament. What a relief! No nasty fleas, but I'm still itchy. A course of antibiotics was prescribed. The way I'm feeling I'd be better with some tranquilisers.

Jane really upset me when she described my recent behaviour as "chandelier-swinging"! I wouldn't mind, but she doesn't have a chandelier, just those sunken ceiling lights! She also complained about my disobedience. The thing is, I'm so worked up all the time. It's hard to sit still, never mind hear what she is asking me to do. I'm not a bad dog, am I?

Really, I'm not one to pop pills, but having finished the course of antibiotics, I'm still scratching and passing wind. My tummy and I are so unhappy, and so is Jane......

In desperation - P.... (F)LEASE, PLEASE HELP ME

Humphrey

My dear Humphrey

You'll be relieved to know that the solution to your problems is simple. The symptoms you describe are a classic reaction to the colours and preservatives in the birthday treats you received from your adoring fan club. It would appear that you are at present clearly *"additive driven"* – so my advice to you is *"ditch the junk food!"*

As humans, we share a significant number of genes with you dogs. Many commercially produced dog foods and treats contain additives *(E numbers)* that are banned in human food. The classic symptoms related to these additives can consist of hyperactivity - in your case, Humphrey, chandelier swingin', restlessness, bulging eyes, inability to listen to your owner *(disobedience),* skin irritation *(itching and scratching)* and digestive upset *(wind – I won't offend your sensibilities by calling it anything else!).*

So if you have an upset tummy or itchy skin, it is most likely to be caused by the food and treats Jane is dishing up to you.

Here's a marvellous website I discovered which rates nearly all the dog foods on the market - do take a look.
www.allaboutdogfood.com

Now then, Humphrey, let's have a look at the ingredients dog food manufacturers use in their recipes.

CEREALS
No Humphrey, not corn flakes or rice crispies!
The "cereals" used can be good or of poor quality and can refer to any sort of grain. It also means the manufacturer can change which cereals are used depending upon which is cheapest at the time.

MEAT AND ANIMAL DERIVATIVES
Yes, my dear dog, I'm sure you want to know which bits of which animal(s), but with such a vague term, just like cereals above, it could be anything – hairy, with or without horns, feathered with beaks and claws – who knows?

FRESH MEAT
This is more like it – good honest protein! Turkey yes, but no Humphrey, it doesn't have to be Christmas!

VEGETABLE PROTEIN EXTRACTS
(or isolate)
Hmm? What veggies and what bits have been extracted and how? I don't like the sound of that either, Mr H.

OILS AND FATS

Let me tell you Humphrey that the dog food chefs know you dogs *love the taste of fat* and guess what? They add extra just to tantalise your taste buds. Goodness knows what has been used and what has been basted........?

DERIVATIVES OF VEGETABLE ORIGIN

You might question what the original vegetable was! The term covers a vast array of possible and changeable ingredients. Good or bad – we can't tell. For the sake of your tummy and skin we'll avoid this lot altogether.

SUGAR BEET PULP

Well, it is said that we all need fibre in our diet. Mind you, too much fibre in our diet can have disastrous side effects! Some schools of thought believe that beet pulp is used as a filler and others are of the opinion it promotes digestive health. It remains a matter of personal preference and you, Humph' may or may not be *"blown away"* by the addition of this fibre to your food.

VEGETABLES

Veggies are very good for us, some more than others. Just like cereals, the term can cover a multitude of good and not so good vegetables.

CHICORY

Now here's an ingredient that not only does you good but tastes good too. The inulin in chicory root can have a positive effect on the bacteria in your tummy and provides soluble fibre. Its taste, my friend, will appeal to your sweet tooth!

VITAMINS AND MINERALS

These vitamins and minerals are exactly the same as those for us humans. They are there to ensure that a dog has everything he needs in his diet. But watch out, Humphrey, some are artificially produced!

ARTIFICIAL PRESERVATIVES AND ANTIOXIDANTS

Time to get technical, Humphrey, so do try to pay attention! Special ingredients are added to prevent food from deteriorating. These can come from natural sources e.g. Vitamin E and Oil of Rosemary. *(No that's not from your friend Rosemary the Bichon Frise in Rover Street!)*

Artificial preservatives do the same job, but have been linked to behaviour, skin and digestive disorders. Even more worryingly, some of these artificial preservatives have been associated with being carcinogenic. Even if there are no scientifically proven or obvious side effects of artificial preservatives and antioxidants, we must question what the insidious and long term physical effects could be.

Waken up Humphrey!

Pass this information to Jane.

It's her responsibility and she will be anxious to make sure she serves you top notch food and treats for a top notch dog!

All the best!

Auntie Rottie x

Freddy

Hilda's Hens

Dear Auntie Rottie

I have just taken on a four month old Border Collie. His name is Freddy. With his previous owners, he was allowed total run of their farm. Here, at his new home, I keep hens.

The problem I'm having with Freddy is that he likes to chase them. He clearly doesn't want to hurt them. I think he just wants to round them up.

In addition to Freddy, I have a Bearded Collie who has never shown the slightest bit of interest in chasing the hens. I have tried rattling the treats tin to get Freddy's attention. Sometimes this works, but more often than not, he doesn't listen!

Help!

Yours hopefully,

Hilda and The Hens

Dear Hilda and the Hens

You are quite right in saying that Freddy is trying to round up your hens. Combine the strong herding instinct of the Border Collie with the freedom Freddy has experienced on the farm, the result is a pup that thinks he can please himself – all the time!

OK Hilda, here's the plan…..

In preparation for this exercise, feed your hens to prevent them mugging you for food when you bring young Freddy into their pen. Freddy must also be hungry. Make sure he is wearing a properly fitted collar from which he cannot back out. Attach a good length of lead. Arm yourself with a bumbag filled with tiny pieces of smoked garlic sausage, cheddar cheese and dried liver – "DOG MONEY"! Retain the value of Freddy's "wages" by only using his "dog money" for training with the hens. Remember, this represents part of his daily food ration and is not a "banker's bonus"!

Not forgetting you, Hilda, make yourself a flask of tea or coffee or whatever you fancy to drink. Alcohol is not recommended as you'll be there for some time! Take your flask and a comfy seat into the hen run. Now bring in young Freddy. Make sure he is aware of your "dog money" and use it to get and reward his attention to you. Sit there for as long as you can - up to an hour, if possible. Repeat daily and more than once, if time allows.

Never take Freddy anywhere near the hens unless he is wearing his collar and lead and you have your "dog money" with you to regain his attention. There's no room for error, Hilda!

Indoors, use a housecage so that Freddy has a safe place to be when you are busy doing other things. This will avoid any chance that he could escape out the back door and terrorise the hens!

Over a period of time, by repeating this routine, he should become accustomed to being near the hens without the need to round them up. This process will take time to achieve. Being consistent is the key.

Finally, you might like to think about acquiring some ducks and teach Freddy to round them up....instead of the hens!

Auntie Rottie

Dennis

Dear Auntie Rottie

I'll come straight to the point! If I don't get my dog Dennis's destructive behaviour sorted out, I will find myself in the divorce courts!

I love the wee rascal but he is costing me a fortune! He chews anything he can get his jaws on! I've had to replace my living room suite after he tore the guts out of it. I've lost count of the number of computer cables he's chewed through. He's ripped up the floor tiles in the kitchen and chewed most of the door frames, not to mention the legs of the piano stool.

The final straw came when Dennis managed to get hold of my husband John's toupee. This has caused untold misery and I've been issued with an ultimatum – it's him or the dog!

Please can you help? I love them both dearly!

Fiona McKay

Dear Fiona

Dare I say, keep your hair on!

I'm so sorry Dennis has caused such disruption and damage and I will do my best to resolve matters for you. I think we should look at the possible reasons for his destructive behaviour.

Dogs chew for many reasons:

Anxiety
Loneliness
Boredom
Discomfort
Insufficient exercise
Insufficient mental stimulation
Habit
In puppies to relieve sore, itchy gums when teething

Reading between the lines, Dennis is not a puppy so we can rule out teething. I suspect that Dennis is a healthy wee fellow but do confirm with your vet that he is physically fit and well. An underlying ailment can lead to this type of inappropriate behaviour.

Now ask yourself a few questions:

Does Dennis have sufficient exercise? How many walks per day does he get? Do you take him for a good interactive walk before you leave him?

Do you leave him with a variety of chew toys? Bear in mind that if toys are always there, they will lose their value and become *"those boring things I've played with for the last month!"*

How long are you leaving Dennis for? Dogs don't have the same conception of time as we do but can still become bored and lonely if left for long periods of time.

Chewing is a stress relieving activity and destruction generally happens within the first 30 minutes of your departure. When you return some time later, please do not punish Dennis for any destruction. He will have no idea why he is being punished. He may look "guilty" but he is only responding to your "angry owner" body language. Punishment will only serve to make him wary of you, especially when your next homecoming is imminent. This can lead to further anxiety and destruction. It then becomes a bit of a vicious circle!

Dennis doesn't need free range of your house. I suggest you purchase a suitable size of housecage for him. No, Fiona, it really isn't cruel to use a cage.

This is about damage limitation and do remember the dog is a denning animal. You can very quickly persuade him that *"this is **the** place to be"* by feeding him in it, giving him tasty treats and chewies in it and, of course, providing him with a luxuriously comfortable bed. Hmm, might be wise to start with an old blanket!

Make sure Dennis's play toys are safe to be left with him, e.g. nylabones, hard rubber rings, etc. Please note that squeaky toys are too easily de-squeaked and cuddly toys easily lose button eyes, etc. and if swallowed can mean an expensive trip to the vet.

Reserve rawhide chews, pigs' ears, etc. as a tasty treat for Dennis to enjoy in his housecage when you are at home and able to supervise their consumption, as they can be quickly eaten and sometimes dogs can choke in their enthusiasm to consume this doggy delicacy.

Once he is accustomed to going into his housecage, do make sure to pop him in there regularly when you are at home. Don't just put him in there when you are going out, for obvious reasons!

Before you leave Dennis, have a really interactive walk together. When you let him off lead, keep changing direction, play hide and seek and praise him lavishly when he finds you and make sure you take some really tasty treats with you to reward him. Smoked garlic sausage is a winner!

Make your departure from the house as calm as possible with no cuddling and fussing – most dogs hate this anyway and if you watch, will no doubt give a big shake off to indicate their dislike of such effusive kowtowing. I suppose it's a bit like being kissed by your mother at the school gate! Oh, the embarrassment! The same applies to your homecoming. Keep it cool. For Dennis, when his pack is split, e.g. you've been out to work, been hunting at the supermarket, etc., it's vital that leadership is re-established. *I'm going to ask you to completely ignore your dog. Yes, I know that appears to be really rude but Dennis is not a furry human, he's a dog.* For him to view you as his leader, you need to be cool, calm and aloof. Certainly when he has calmed down, call him to you and tell him how much you have missed him. In the meantime, I suggest you make a huge fuss of your husband John – it may stand you in good stead!

There is a toy on the market called a Kong. There are various models available but those I like to use are hollow rubber domes, a bit like old-fashioned beehives, which can be simply or ingeniously stuffed depending upon your dog's excavation skills. Too easy – and the Kong is emptied in record time. Too difficult – and the dog gives up! It's a good idea to invest in two giant Kongs for maximum and lasting enjoyment.

Let's get stuffed!
Smear the inside of your Kongs with peanut butter, tubey cheese (Primula) or left over pate or even some tinned dog meat. Then pack in some of Dennis's food, mixed with tiny pieces of cheese, sausage, carrot, apple, etc. Complete with a scrummy lid of peanut butter or tubey cheese, etc. As Dennis becomes more skilful in excavating his Kongs, you need to become more skilful in stuffing them! You can soak some of his food in chicken or beef stock which dogs find heavenly and stuff the Kongs with it. Even put the Kongs in the freezer overnight for maximum effect. Just before you go out the door, present Dennis with his culinary delights – and *go*!

Remember, the contents of Dennis's Kongs are part of his daily ration and not overtime or a bonus. Upon your return remove his Kongs to make them ready for next time. Remember to winkle out those really tasty bits Dennis couldn't quite reach – it makes for a really pleasant homecoming - after you've done the ignoring bit to re-establish your leadership, of course! By only giving stuffed Kongs when you go out and at no other time, you will teach your dog to really look forward to being left alone.

When you **are** at home, keep the doors *closed* so that Dennis does not have access to the whole house and its contents thus preventing any interior alterations he may wish to make! If his antics can't be supervised, I suggest you put him into his housecage.

Don't leave *"Dennis Magnets"* lying around and might I suggest that John keeps his toupee in a drawer or on his head!

If all else fails, you might need to get yourself a good divorce lawyer!

Good luck!

Auntie Rottie

Dear Auntie Rottie

We have just adopted a 6 month old Border Terrier bitch, Judy. She came from a home where both owners worked fulltime. It is obvious they didn't realise what a huge commitment it is having a dog. She is somewhat overweight, but we are very strict with her daily rations and she has regular exercise.

The real problem we have is that Judy likes to shred paper – any paper: newspapers, loo rolls, tissues, paper in waste paper baskets – in fact, any paper she can get her jaws on.

Last week, in preparation for renewing our car's road tax, my husband, George, left the registration document and money on the kitchen counter. He left the kitchen for 2 minutes to get his jacket and the car keys and upon his return discovered Judy surrounded by the shredded registration document. The money (£10 notes) was strewn across the floor but to our amazement was completely undamaged – not a tooth mark! Why would that be?

Very sheepishly, George took the shredded document
to the Post Office where the marvellous assistant was
able to piece together the bar code! All was not lost
and he proffered the miraculously undamaged notes
in payment of the road tax.

Judy has loads of toys, chew bones, etc., but would
exchange them all for PAPER! Although she appears
to love her housecage, we don't want to leave her in it
all the time, as that is what her previous owners did.

Help!

"In Shreds"

Dear "In Shreds" and George

Judy is being a puppy – doing what puppies do! Shredding paper is great fun! It's a bit like very young children at Christmas or birthdays that prefer to play with the packaging rather than its contents!

Judy's previous owners kept her in a housecage for long periods of time because they were out working. As a result of this, Judy will have missed out on some of the very important developmental stages of puppyhood. With little or no mental stimulation, she will have been very bored. I suspect she is making up for lost time!

Judy is still very young and, just like a toddler, she shouldn't be left unsupervised. So please don't feel guilty about putting her in her housecage when you are unable to observe and supervise what she is doing. Do remember the dog is a denning animal. So, even if you only want to go to the loo or hang out the washing or hoover the bedrooms, put Judy in her housecage. It's her safe place, her den.

Many people believe it's cruel to shut their dog in a housecage, but isn't it worse to allow a dog to be destructive (it can happen in a nanosecond!) and then punish them for a behaviour that may have occurred sometime earlier?

Puppies, like babies, explore everything with their mouths. *"It's all chew toys to the dog"* – even your best Gucci loafers if you happen to be fortunate enough to own a pair! Could you ever forgive yourself if Judy chewed an electric cable and found herself wired to the National Grid?

Stating the obvious – ha! Don't leave papers lying around, shut the bathroom door(s), bedroom door(s), dispose of paper directly to the recycling bin rather than putting it in a waste paper basket!

When you need to go out for any length of time, put Judy in her housecage with a stuffed Kong. Refer to the advice I gave Denis's owner in the article entitled Destructive Dennis.

Interestingly, dogs spend on average 17 hours per day either asleep or resting (I wish I was a dog!).

As a guide, Judy may be **out** of her housecage:

When she is being exercised.

During short play-train sessions.

When you and she are attending your local reputable dog training group.

When she is going outside to toilet.

When you are able to keep a close eye on her.

If you don't know where Judy is *at all times* she needs to be in her housecage.

You may not need to use the housecage forever, but you'll find that Judy will look upon it as her own den, just like you with your favourite comfy armchair!

With best wishes

Auntie Rottie

P.S.I don't know why Judy didn't chew up the money. Count yourselves lucky! Maybe she smelled it, thought "filthy lucre"! I'm sure Judy's preference would be for "Dog Money" aka treats!

Dear Auntie Rottie

This morning, as usual, I left my dog named Zak tied up outside the local newsagent. Zak is a stunning 12 month old German Shepherd. As I was waiting to collect my newspaper, I happened to glance outside and to my horror a man was trying to untie Zak's lead. I shouted and dashed outside and the man ran away up the street. I was terrified he might have been able to steal my wonderful Zak.

Immediately, I reported this incident to the police. They alerted me that there is a high incidence of dog theft in the area and that it would be virtually impossible to find the man I described.

Zak is the first dog I have ever owned. I have worked hard at training and socialising him and he is a very well behaved and friendly dog. It would break my heart if anything happened to him!

Is there anything I can teach Zak that would deter a potential thief? As I don't intend breeding with him, my vet has advised I have Zak neutered and I plan to have him microchipped at the same time. Is there anything else I can do?

Thank you.

From "an alarmed owner", Sally

Zak

Dear Sally

You can't train Zak to recognise, never mind deter, a thief!

You can't teach him "stranger danger"!

You wouldn't leave a toddler tied up outside a shop – would you?

There's nothing you can teach Zak to prevent him going with a stranger, yet still be a socially safe dog with other people!

#51536840

Please don't leave your young dog, or any age of dog for that matter, unsupervised in public. Dog theft is a rife and lucrative business. Many dogs are stolen from their own back gardens! Dogs can be stolen to order just because they happen to be a popular breed or to be sold to laboratories, or to dog fighting rings that use them as "bait" dogs. These dogs are rarely traced.

There are a lot of odd people out there who could do cruel and wicked things to your dog. Bear in mind, those same people would not hesitate to report your dog as aggressive. Be warned! Keep Zak safe!

Microchipping is an excellent idea in case your dog gets lost, but may be of little or no use if your dog is stolen.

Best wishes

Auntie Rottie

Don't leave them alone!

In Parked Cars   Outside Shops

The Incident of the Bubble-gum Machine

One bright sunny Saturday morning Jennifer G and her Golden Retriever by the name of Max walked up to their local shop. Outside the shop was a large bubble-gum machine to which Max, as per usual, was fastened.

Whilst Jennifer was in the shop, a motorbike roared up the street, back-firing as it sped past. In a state of sheer panic, Max shot to the end of his lead pulling the bubble-gum machine over. In his efforts to escape, it appeared to poor Max that the bubble-gum machine was chasing him down the street!

To further Max's predicament, a customer coming out of the shop rushed to the rescue. Instead of trying to release the dog's lead from the bubble-gum machine, he tried to grab the dog in an attempt to cut short his flight. Unfortunately, this served to further panic the already terrified Max.

On hearing the commotion, Jennifer G dashed to the shop door. A scene of carnage lay before her. Max and the man were flailing around on the ground – the dog trying to escape from the man and the bubble-gum machine – and the man attempting to pin the dog down in an effort to restrain him. The bubble-gum machine had burst open surrounding the hapless pair in a sea of tiny coloured balls.

Jennifer G's efforts to intervene were somewhat hampered by the balls of bubble-gum acting like ball bearings under her feet as she slipped and skidded across the pavement.

With some difficulty, she managed to convince the man to let go of Max and to turn his attentions to releasing the dog's lead from the bubble-gum machine.

By this time Max's "super hero" was puce in the face, sweating profusely and extremely flustered. He tripped over the coloured bubble-gum balls and shot headlong across to the bubble-gum machine. With a herculean effort he was able to extricate the dog's lead. Given the circumstances, this was no mean feat, as, when the dog first tried to escape, the impetus had pulled the knot so tight it was almost impossible to untie.

Of course, such uproar had attracted a crowd of onlookers, each one offering different advice to the beleaguered dog and owner. Having suddenly realised he was free of the bubble-gum machine, Max, in desperation, dragged his owner down the street, making for home as fast as his legs could carry him, leaving a trail of devastation behind him.

On arrival home both Jennifer and Max were in a state of shock. With trembling hands, a sobbing Jennifer brewed a pot of tea and sat down. Max had disappeared to his bed and turned his back on the world. Jennifer could only imagine how Max might be feeling after such an ordeal and telephoned her vet for advice. She was advised to keep Max quiet and to contact her trainer.

It was some considerable time later that day, when Jennifer and Max had calmed down sufficiently, that Jennifer felt she could leave Max at home so that she could return to the scene of the "crime" and apologise to the owner of the shop.

Although the bubble-gum machine was wrecked, the shopkeeper had actually done quite well out of the whole incident. The crowd of onlookers had all bought bits and pieces in the shop while they discussed the morning's events. Max's "super hero" had disappeared so Jennifer put a thank-you card in the window on Max's and her behalf.

Poor Max was a shadow of his former self. This placid dog, who didn't have much confidence in the first place, became a virtual recluse. He refused to walk up the street, was terrified of men and of any loud noise and attempted to bolt anytime he happened to see anything vaguely resembling a bubble-gum machine.

It took months of careful rehabilitation with help from their professional trainer, before Max could be walked up the street , past their local shop, be relaxed around men and not freak out at the sight of an object that looked like a bubble-gum machine. Motor bikes, however, are still an issue......

The moral of the story? Never leave your dog tied up outside a shop and certainly not tied to a bubble-gum machine!

That's all for now folks!